Once upon a time, there was an old clock shop. Inside the shop lived a whole flock of clocks. There were alarm clocks, cuckoo clocks, even a tall grandfather clock.

1

All day long, the shop was filled with the sound of clocks. "Tick, tock. Tick, tock. Tick, tock." But one clock stood out from the rest. His name was Tick.

Tick had a problem.
"Tick, tick. Tick, tick. Tick, tick."
Tick was a clock who could not tock!

"What poppycock!" said Grandfather Clock.
"All clocks can tock. You must simply try harder."
Tick tried with all his might. But it was no use.
He just couldn't tock.

The other clocks began to tease Tick. "What good is a clock who can't tock?" they said. Tick hated being a laughing stock, but what could he do?

Then late one day, as the shopkeeper was
about to lock up, there was a knock at the door.
In walked a woman carrying a pink clock.

The woman handed the clock to the shopkeeper.
"I don't like this clock," she said. "Perhaps you
can sell it to someone else."

The next morning, the clocks welcomed the new member of their flock. But they were in for quite a shock. When the clock opened her mouth, out came, "Tock, tock. Tock, tock. Tock, tock."

Tick couldn't believe it—a clock who could only tock! This gave Tick an idea. He whispered something to Tock, the new clock.

Then the two clocks stood up tall, side by side.
In perfect time came the sound of each clock,
"Tick, tock. Tick, tock. Tick, tock."

A customer heard the musical tick-tocking of the two clocks working together. "How lovely!" he said. "I've never seen anything like that before." Tick was as proud as a peacock. So was Tock.

The customer bought Tick and Tock.
"I'll have the most unusual clocks
on my block!" he said.

So Tick and Tock went home with the man.
There, the two friends ticked and tocked
around the clock and lived happily
ever after.

-ock Word Family Riddles

Listen to the riddle sentences. Add the right letter or letters to the -ock sound to finish each one.

 1   To find out the time I look at the ____ock.

 2   My toe was cold because there was a hole in my __ock.

 3   He got paint on this shirt because he did not wear an art ____ock.

 4   Do not touch the plug or you will get an electric ____ock.

5   At the door I heard someone ____ock.

6 The boat is anchored to the ___ock.

7 While hiking I stubbed my toe on a ___ock.

8 Only I know the combination to my bicycle ___ock.

9 To finish the tower we need one more building ____ock.

10 A group of bees is called a swarm. A group of birds is called a ____ock.

Now make up some new riddle sentences using - ock

Give a great holler, a cheer, a yell

For all of the words that we can spell

With an O, C, and K that make the sound –ock,

You'll find it in tock and block and clock.

Three little letters, that's all that we need

To make a whole family of words to read!

Make a list of other –ock words. Then use them in the cheer!